# Highlights®
# DINOSAURS
## Giants of the Earth

## By Dougal Dixon

# CONTENTS

The Dinosaur series was created for Highlights for Children, Inc. by Bender Richardson White, P.O. Box 266, Uxbridge UB9 5NX, England

Printed in the USA

Project Editor: Lionel Bender
Art Director: Ben White
Production: Kim Richardson
Assistant Editor: Madeleine Samuel
Typesetting and Media Conversion: Peter MacDonald & Una Macnamara

Educational Advisor: Andrew Gutelle
Production Coordinator: Sarah Robinson

10 9 8 7 6 5 4 3

**The Age of Dinosaurs**
The first dinosaurs appeared about 225 million years ago (mya for short) in what scientists call the Late Triassic Period. They thrived through the following Jurassic Period and died out at the end of the Cretaceous Period 65 million years ago. During this time, geography, climate, and vegetation, or plant life, were constantly changing—as shown in these dinosaur scenes.

**Triassic 245–208 mya**
A single giant landmass or supercontinent, mostly desert conditions, tree ferns, and conifers.

**Early and Middle Jurassic 208–157 mya** Supercontinent, shallow seas, moist climate, tree ferns, conifers, and cycads.

# INTRODUCTION

When we look at a dinosaur skeleton in a museum, at a dinosaur model in a display, or at a dinosaur picture in a book, we are at first amazed by the strangeness of the creature. We wonder that such an incredible beast could exist at all. Then, when we begin to read about dinosaurs, and to understand them and how they lived, we begin to ask questions.

Where did the dinosaurs come from? What kind of world did they live in? How long did they exist?

These are all questions that scientists have been trying to answer for more than 160 years. Some answers to them come from the rocks in which dinosaur bones are found. The kinds of rocks can tell us about the landscapes of the past—for instance, sandstones that formed in huge ancient deserts, shale and mudstones from deep, wide, muddy rivers, and limestones that formed in lime-rich seas millions of years ago.

The remains of living creatures that we find in the rocks are called fossils, and these can tell us about the dinosaurs' surroundings. Plant fossils show us the vegetation, and animal fossils show us the other creatures that lived at the same time.

The fossils from rocks dating from before the Age of Dinosaurs can give us a picture of life on Earth up to that time. We can work out the evolution of the dinosaurs from the different kinds of animals that existed earlier.

We still do not have all the answers about dinosaurs, and every fresh discovery tells us something new. However, slowly over the years we have been building up a picture of these magnificent creatures of the past, and of their world.

**Late Jurassic 157–146 mya**
Supercontinent beginning to break up, dry inland, moist climates by coasts.

**Early Cretaceous 146–97 mya**
Continents drifting into separate landmasses, plant life as in Triassic and Jurassic periods.

**Late Cretaceous 97–65 mya**
Separate continents, each with its own animal life, and plants like modern types.

# DINOSAUR PARADE BEGINS

Here they come! A parade of the animals that lived on Earth between the Late Triassic Period, about 225 million years ago, and the end of the Cretaceous Period, about 65 million years ago.

At the beginning, in the Triassic, there were all kinds of reptiles—running reptiles, swimming reptiles, digging reptiles, even flying reptiles. (There were also the first mammals. Those were small, shrewlike animals.) Among the reptiles were some crocodile-like animals, each with a long tail and strong hind legs. Scientists call these creatures the thecodonts. They became great in number when the other types of reptiles died out, and their descendants—the animals that evolved from them—took up many kinds of lifestyles. As they did so, they developed bodily shapes to suit their behavior. One group of thecodonts began to walk about on their strong hind legs, holding their long tails out behind them to balance. These animals became the first dinosaurs. The earliest dinosaurs were nimble little hunting animals not much different from their thecodont ancestors, the creatures they evolved from.

▷ In the parade of Triassic and Early Jurassic animals we can see the first of the dinosaurs emerging. These included meat- eaters like *Staurikosaurus* and *Coelophysis*, long-necked plant-eaters like *Anchisaurus* and *Plateosaurus*, and two-footed plant-eaters— those that moved around on just their hind legs— like *Fabrosaurus* and *Heterodontosaurus*.

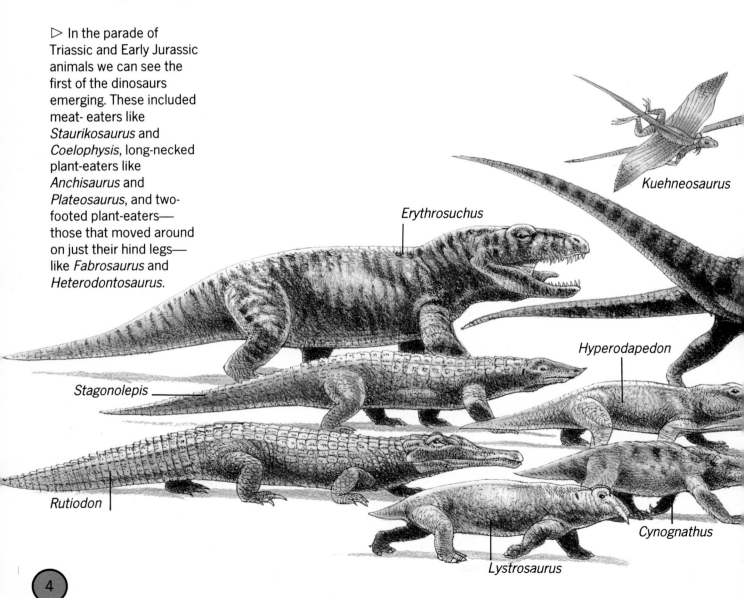

Kuehneosaurus

Erythrosuchus

Hyperodapedon

Stagonolepis

Rutiodon

Lystrosaurus

Cynognathus

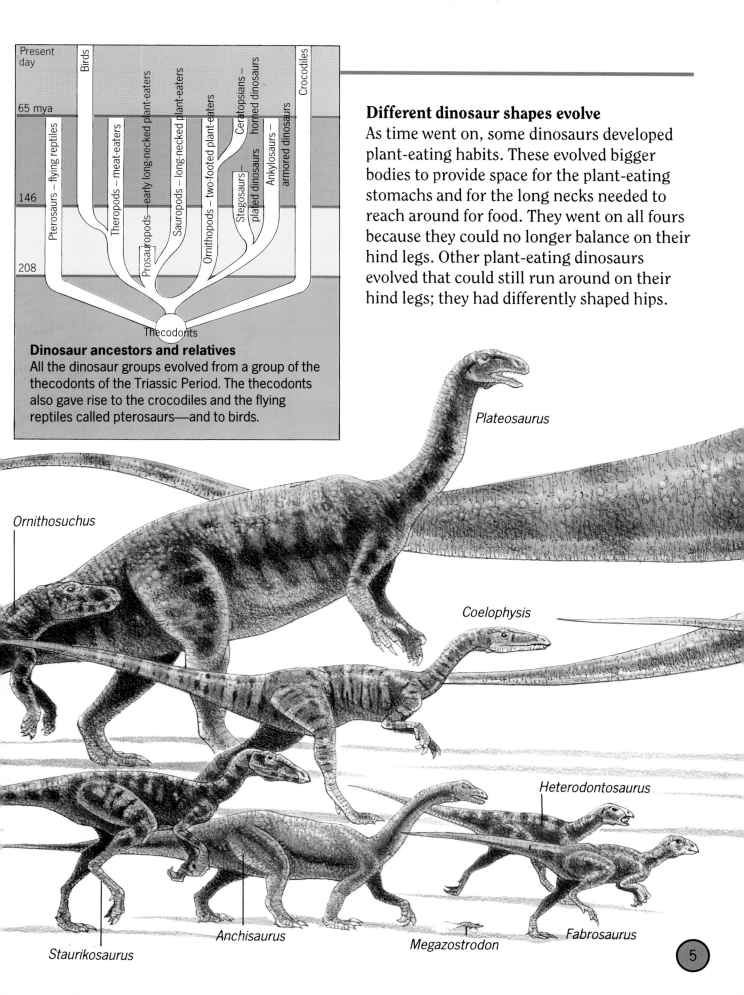

| Present day | | | | | | | | | |
|---|---|---|---|---|---|---|---|---|---|

Birds

Pterosaurs – flying reptiles

Theropods – meat-eaters

Prosauropods—early long-necked plant-eaters

Sauropods – long-necked plant-eaters

Ornithopods – two-footed plant-eaters

Stegosaurs – plated dinosaurs

Ceratopsians – horned dinosaurs

Ankylosaurs – armored dinosaurs

Crocodiles

65 mya

146

208

Thecodonts

**Dinosaur ancestors and relatives**

All the dinosaur groups evolved from a group of the thecodonts of the Triassic Period. The thecodonts also gave rise to the crocodiles and the flying reptiles called pterosaurs—and to birds.

### Different dinosaur shapes evolve

As time went on, some dinosaurs developed plant-eating habits. These evolved bigger bodies to provide space for the plant-eating stomachs and for the long necks needed to reach around for food. They went on all fours because they could no longer balance on their hind legs. Other plant-eating dinosaurs evolved that could still run around on their hind legs; they had differently shaped hips.

Plateosaurus

Ornithosuchus

Coelophysis

Heterodontosaurus

Staurikosaurus

Anchisaurus

Megazostrodon

Fabrosaurus

# DINOSAURS MARCH ON

The parade of dinosaurs continues in the Jurassic Period. This was the greatest time of the dinosaurs. The desert conditions of the Triassic gave way to moister climates in the Jurassic as shallow seas spread over the continents. All sorts of new dinosaurs evolved to live in the woodlands and forests of the new environments.

The swift-moving little meat-eaters were still around, but there were also huge, dragonlike meat-eaters. These great killers evolved to feed upon the plant-eaters that had also grown huge. The long-necked four-footed plant-eaters were the largest land animals that ever lived. The two-footed plant-eaters continued, too, and some of these developed into armored types—great heavy beasts that also had gone back to a four-footed way of life.

The skies were dominated by the flying reptiles, the pterosaurs, but the true birds evolved at the end of the Jurassic Period. The small mammals still scuttled around, but had not developed into any particularly special creatures.

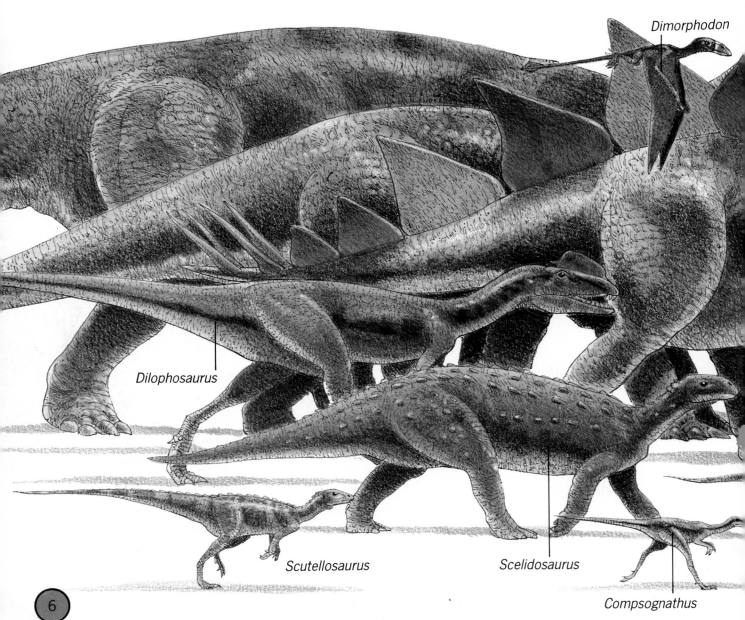

Dimorphodon

Dilophosaurus

Scutellosaurus

Scelidosaurus

Compsognathus

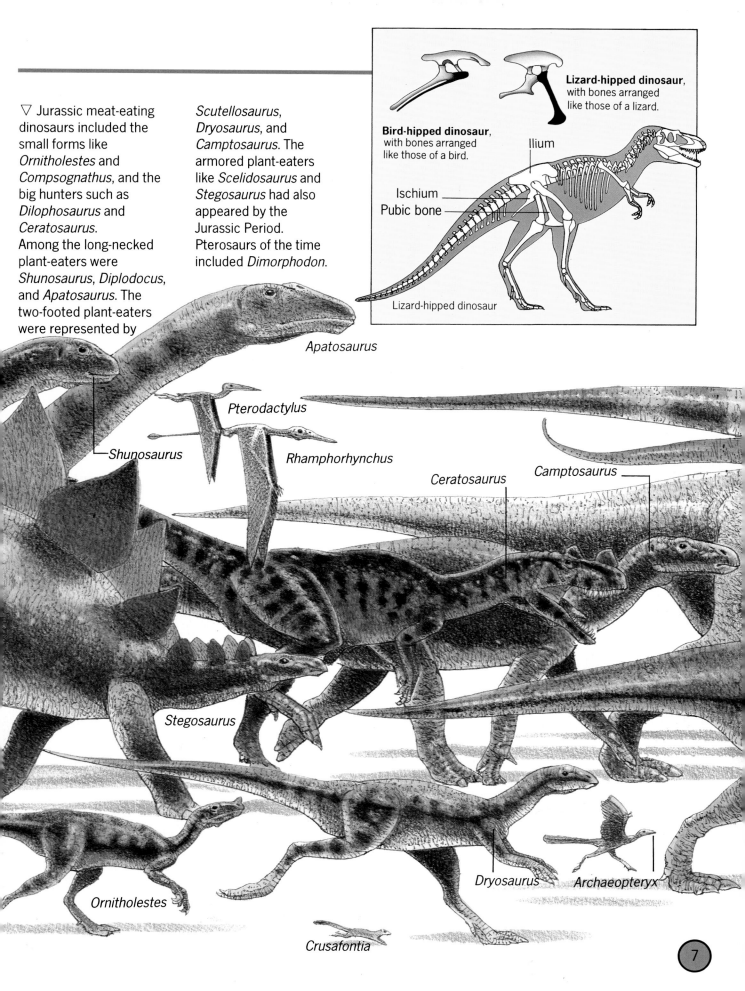

▽ Jurassic meat-eating dinosaurs included the small forms like *Ornitholestes* and *Compsognathus*, and the big hunters such as *Dilophosaurus* and *Ceratosaurus*. Among the long-necked plant-eaters were *Shunosaurus*, *Diplodocus*, and *Apatosaurus*. The two-footed plant-eaters were represented by *Scutellosaurus*, *Dryosaurus*, and *Camptosaurus*. The armored plant-eaters like *Scelidosaurus* and *Stegosaurus* had also appeared by the Jurassic Period. Pterosaurs of the time included *Dimorphodon*.

**Bird-hipped dinosaur**, with bones arranged like those of a bird.

**Lizard-hipped dinosaur**, with bones arranged like those of a lizard.

Ilium

Ischium

Pubic bone

Lizard-hipped dinosaur

*Apatosaurus*

*Shunosaurus*

*Pterodactylus*

*Rhamphorhynchus*

*Ceratosaurus*

*Camptosaurus*

*Stegosaurus*

*Dryosaurus*

*Archaeopteryx*

*Ornitholestes*

*Crusafontia*

# DINOSAUR PARADE ENDS

By the time the parade arrives in the Cretaceous Period, it has reached the peak of dinosaur development. Along with the small and big meat-eaters, the long-necked and the two-footed plant-eaters, we also find new kinds of armored dinosaurs including bizarre horned types.

Up to this point the same types of dinosaurs had lived all over the world. Now we are seeing different types appearing on different continents. A type of two-footed plant-eater was widespread in North America, while the long-necked plant-eaters continued to be most important in South America.

Then, at the end of the Cretaceous, just as they were becoming really spectacular, the dinosaurs suddenly vanished. The parade came to a halt. And along with the dinosaurs went the pterosaurs and other great reptile types of the time. It was the little mammals that continued. So unimportant throughout the Age of Dinosaurs, they survived the reptiles and went on to produce their own parade that brings us up to the present day.

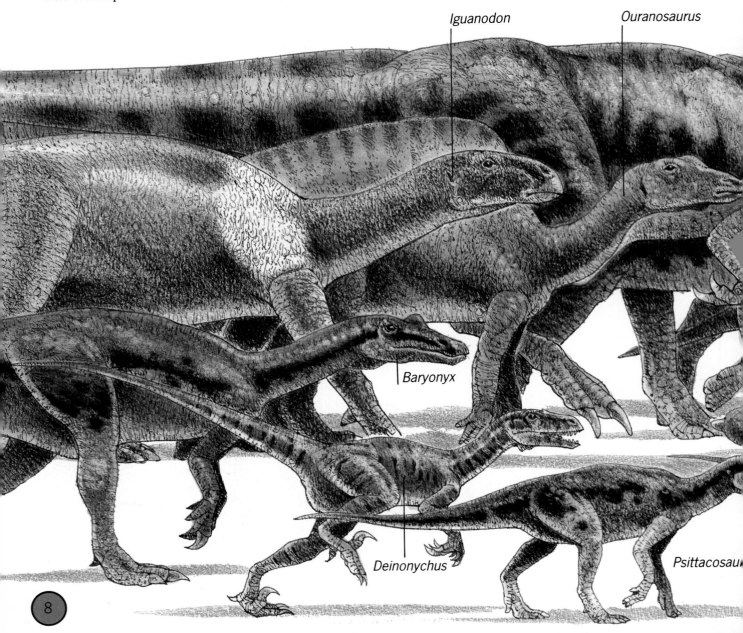

*Iguanodon*

*Ouranosaurus*

*Baryonyx*

*Deinonychus*

*Psittacosau*

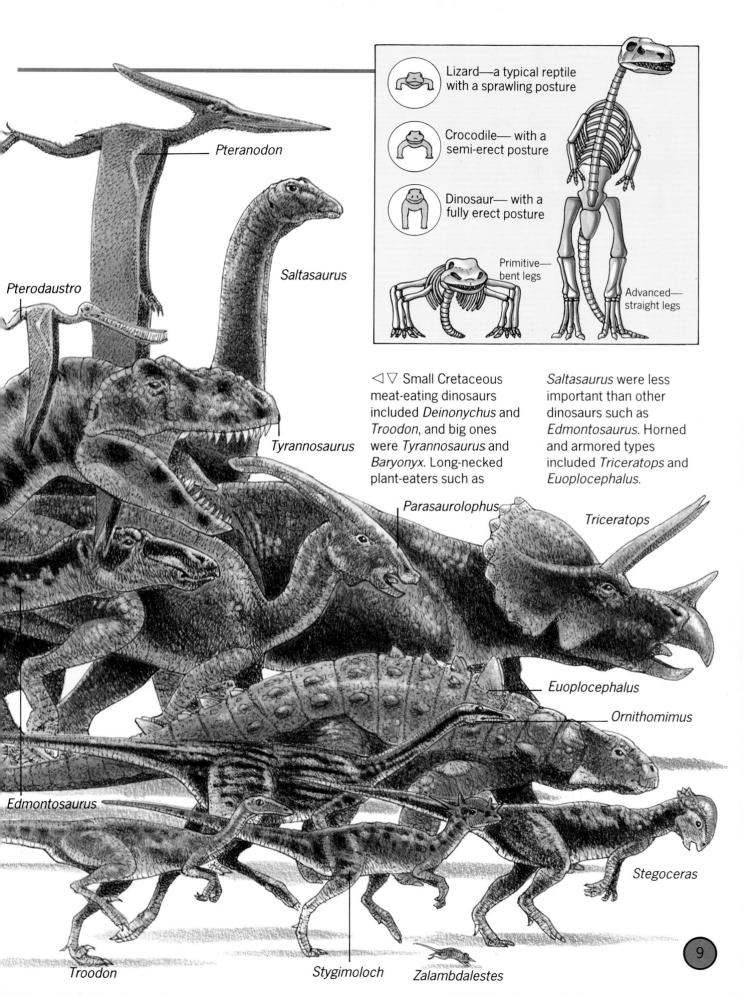

Pteranodon

Saltasaurus

Pterodaustro

Lizard—a typical reptile with a sprawling posture

Crocodile— with a semi-erect posture

Dinosaur— with a fully erect posture

Primitive— bent legs

Advanced— straight legs

Tyrannosaurus

◁▽ Small Cretaceous meat-eating dinosaurs included *Deinonychus* and *Troodon*, and big ones were *Tyrannosaurus* and *Baryonyx*. Long-necked plant-eaters such as

*Saltasaurus* were less important than other dinosaurs such as *Edmontosaurus*. Horned and armored types included *Triceratops* and *Euoplocephalus*.

Parasaurolophus

Triceratops

Euoplocephalus

Ornithomimus

Edmontosaurus

Stegoceras

Troodon

Stygimoloch

Zalambdalestes

# THE TIME SCALE OF EVOLUTION

It has taken the Earth a long time to get to where it is today—about 4.6 thousand million years, in fact. At first the Earth was a ball of hot molten rock. Then it started to cool down. There have probably been living things of some sort present on Earth as long as its surface has been solid and cool enough to support them.

At first, life forms would only have been made up of molecules of matter that could reproduce, or make copies of, themselves. Any change to these molecules that would have improved their chances of reproduction would be carried on to the next molecules: their offspring or children. Then the whole machinery of evolution would have been set in motion. Evolution is a process by which new kinds, or species, of living things develop from others.

These early forms of life left no remains, or fossils, and for about seven-eighths of the Earth's history we have only the vaguest idea of what types of living things were around.

▽ The evolution of, or changes to, the surface of the Earth, from the time it started to cool until the present day. Each level of the folded band covers a little more than 1,000 million years.

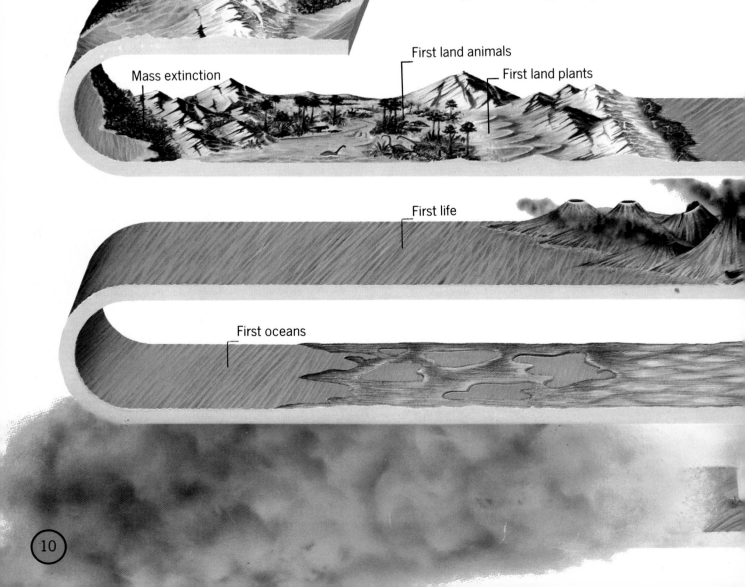

Ice age

Mass extinction

First land animals

First land plants

First life

First oceans

Then, 570 million years ago, animals with hard shells evolved. These produced fossils. From that time we have a clearer picture of how life developed. At first all creatures lived in the sea. But about 420 million years ago, plants and animals began to grow on the land. Some fish left the water and evolved into amphibians, of which present-day frogs and toads are examples. From these, the reptiles evolved. The period of time between 245 and 65 million years ago is known as the Age of Reptiles. Within this period was the time of dinosaurs. When the big reptiles vanished, the Age of Mammals began, and this has lasted to the present day.

## Geological periods

Geology is the study of the Earth's rocks. Geological time, the Earth's lifespan, is so long that scientists find it helpful to divide it up into sections called periods. Each period is marked by the kinds of animals that existed at that time, and hence on the fossils that we find in the rocks laid down then. The dinosaurs lived in the Age of Reptiles—the Triassic, Jurassic, and Cretaceous periods. [All dates in the chart are in millions of years ago.]

**Holocene 0.01-0**
Modern times.

**Pleistocene 1.64-0.01**
Ice-age mammals including early humans.

**Pliocene 5.2-1.64**
Cool climates. Mammal life similar to present day.

**Miocene 23.5-5.2**
Mountain ranges form. Widespread grass-eating, running mammals.

**Oligocene 35.5-23.5**
Cool climate. Mammals beginning to look like modern types.

**Eocene 56.5-35.5**
Forests. Mammals widespread.

**Paleocene 65-56.5**
Forests. All kinds of new mammals develop.

**Cretaceous 146-65**
Forests, then shallow seas. Last of the dinosaurs.

**Jurassic 208-146**
Shallow seas, wooded islands. First birds.

**Triassic 245-208**
Dry land with deserts. First dinosaurs and mammals.

**Permian 290-245**
Mountains and deserts. Reptiles dominate the land.

**Carboniferous 363-290**
Seas, swamps, then ice. First reptiles.

**Devonian 409-363**
Mountains and lakes. First amphibians.

**Silurian 439-409**
Ice caps over seas, then open seas. First land plants.

**Ordovician 510-439**
Dry land without plants, then seas. First fish.

**Cambrian 570-510**
Widespread seas. First shelled animals.

**Precambrian 4,600-570**
Shallow seas. Only simple life.

First hard-shelled animals

First traces of oxygen in atmosphere

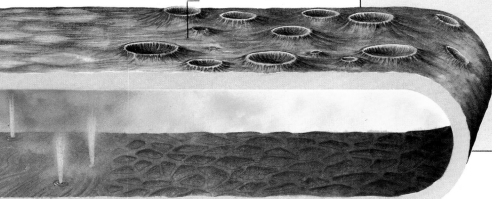
Earth cooling

4,600
Precambrian

# THE MOVING WORLD

**360–286 mya**
In the Carboniferous Period, most of the continents of the time (gray areas) were joined together, and the rest were drifting toward this great landmass.

**245–208 mya**
In the Triassic Period, when the dinosaurs first appeared, the continents were jammed together to form a supercontinent, called Pangaea.

**208–146 mya**
During the Jurassic Period, Pangaea was still one single continent, but it was beginning to split. Shallow seas flooded over much of it.

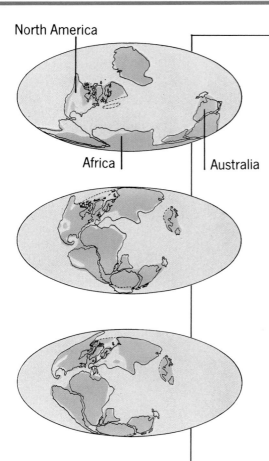

North America

Africa

Australia

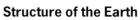

We live, and the dinosaurs lived, in a world that is constantly changing.

The surface of the land is continually being worn away by the action of the rain, rivers, glaciers, wind, and all other kinds of natural processes. Over millions of years, mountains are worn down to rubble and sand, which are carried away by streams and rivers and dumped on plains and in oceans. There they form rocks, which can be folded up into new mountains and added to the continents.

Not only that, but the very structure of the continents is changing. And the continents are slowly moving about over the surface of the Earth. Our planet consists of a number of layers—the core, the mantle, and the crust. The crust and a solid part of the mantle below it form giant plates on the Earth's surface.

**Structure of the Earth**
The mantle forms the largest portion of the Earth. Movements in the mantle, in which molten rock material rises and spreads out and cool rock material sinks, are responsible for the movement of the Earth's outer layers. The top layer is called the crust. It is the Earth's skin.

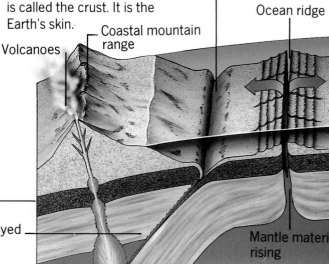

Ocean plate sliding beneath continental plate

Ocean ridge

Coastal mountain range

Volcanoes

Margin where plate destroyed

Mantle materi rising

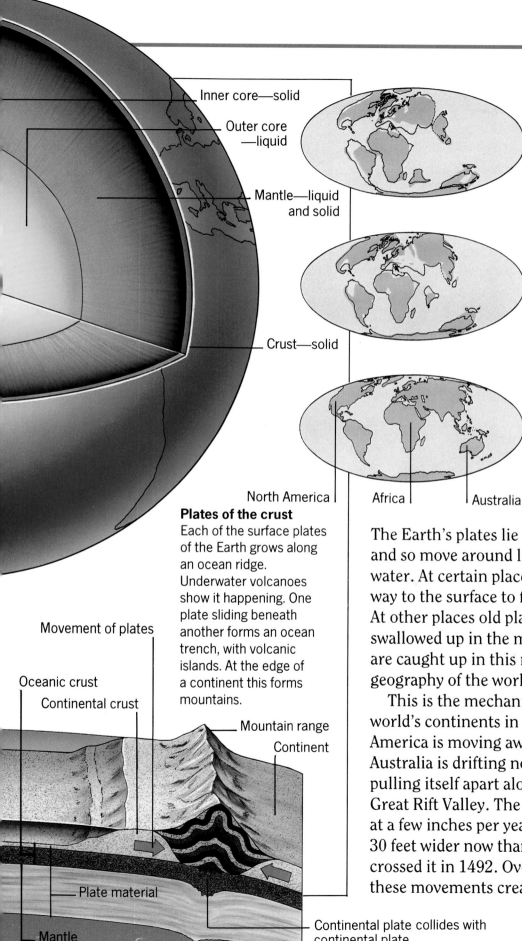

Inner core—solid

Outer core—liquid

Mantle—liquid and solid

Crust—solid

**146–65 mya**
In the Cretaceous Period, the end of the dinosaurs' time, Pangaea had mostly broken up into chunks that we would recognize as the modern continents.

**65–52 mya**
During the Tertiary Period, the Age of Mammals, the continents were drifting toward the positions in which they find themselves today.

**Modern times**
Today's pattern of continents is temporary. The continents are still drifting, and in times to come the world map will be different again.

North America | Africa | Australia

**Plates of the crust**
Each of the surface plates of the Earth grows along an ocean ridge. Underwater volcanoes show it happening. One plate sliding beneath another forms an ocean trench, with volcanic islands. At the edge of a continent this forms mountains.

Movement of plates

Oceanic crust

Continental crust

Mountain range

Continent

Plate material

Mantle

Continental plate collides with continental plate

The Earth's plates lie on a soft layer of mantle and so move around like leaves floating on water. At certain places molten rock forces its way to the surface to form new plate material. At other places old plate material melts and is swallowed up in the mantle. The continents are caught up in this movement and so the geography of the world constantly changes.

This is the mechanism that keeps the world's continents in motion. At the moment America is moving away from Europe, Australia is drifting northward, and Africa is pulling itself apart along a split called the Great Rift Valley. The movements take place at a few inches per year. The Atlantic Ocean is 30 feet wider now than it was when Columbus crossed it in 1492. Over millions of years, these movements create even bigger changes.

# AT THE BEGINNING

The first part of the history of life on our planet—the time known as the Precambrian Era—is very unclear. All living things had soft bodies and left few fossils for us to study. Then, in the Cambrian Period, animals developed shells and horny coverings. These are the kinds of things we often find as fossils. We do not know why this change happened. Maybe the chemicals in the seawater changed and allowed animals to grow hard parts. Anyway, from the Cambrian Period onward, the rocks are full of fossils and we can trace the evolution of life with some confidence.

In telling the dinosaur story, two events were very important: the development of vertebrates, and the colonization of land. The first vertebrates—animals with backbones—were the fish. These evolved from wormlike creatures that had a stiff rod supporting a long body.

### Early life forms
The first living creatures had just one cell. They must have resembled some modern blue-green algae. In modern waters mats of blue-green algae trap mud and build up lumps called stromatolites like the ones in this photo. Fossil stromatolites are known from Precambrian rocks.

Single-cell blue-green algae

### Cambrian Period 570–510 million years ago
The first common fossils are found in Cambrian rocks. These are of spongelike and wormlike sea creatures, and of the first animals with hard shells.

### Ordovician Period 510–439 million years ago
The first fish evolved in the Ordovician Period, but the more common fossils are of lampshells, nautilus-like animals, trilobites, and sea lilies.

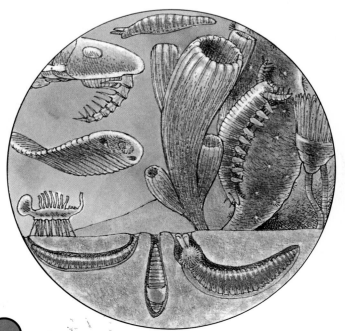

In the early fish, the stiff rod became divided into sections, making it flexible like a chain. Flaps evolved at each side of the body to allow swimming. And the brain at the front of the animal became encased in a box, the skull, for protection. The basic fish shape, with a backbone, fins, and skull, had evolved by Devonian times.

For most of the Earth's history the atmosphere—the air around it—had been a mixture of poisonous gases. Along with the first primitive animals in the sea, the first primitive plants evolved. Plants live by using sunlight as energy to make their food. They give off oxygen as a product of this. While life existed only in the sea, oxygen had been bubbling up from the seaweed and other primitive plants. Eventually, by the Silurian Period, there was enough oxygen in the atmosphere to support life out of the water.

**Silurian Period 439–409 million years ago**
Common fossils of the Silurian Period include trilobites and corals. Fossils of the first land-living creatures of this time are rare.

**Devonian Period 409–363 million years ago**
By Devonian times, land life was doing well, but in the sea fish had become very common. The Devonian Period is called the Age of Fish.

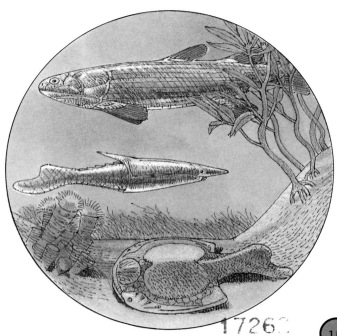

# BEFORE DINOSAURS

The first vertebrate to live on land was most likely a kind of fish, like the lungfish today. It would have had a lung, so it could breathe air as we do, and paired muscular fins, so it could pull itself over land. It would have been able to live on land for only short periods. This may have allowed it to survive when ponds dried out in dry seasons, or to hunt the insects and spiders that were already living on land.

In Devonian times the first amphibians evolved. These were much like the lungfish. They still had a head and tail like those of a fish. But they also had strong ribs to work the lungs, and proper legs with toes. Some could live out of the water for long periods, yet still had to return to the water to lay eggs.

The Carboniferous Period was a time of rivers with broad deltas and swamps, ideal places for amphibians. All kinds evolved. But the first reptiles developed at this time as well.

*Westlothiana*

**Carboniferous Period 363 million years ago**
The Carboniferous coal forests were filled with amphibians and insects, and were also home to the first reptile, *Westlothiana*, shown here.

Edaphosaurus     Dimetrodon

Diplocaulus

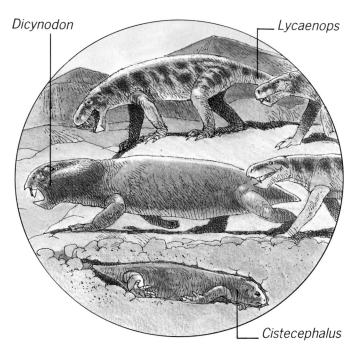

Dicynodon     Lycaenops

Cistecephalus

**Permian Period 290 million years ago**
Amphibians flourished in the oases of the Permian deserts, but more successful were reptiles like the herd-living *Edaphosaurus* and *Dimetrodon*, a hunter.

△ The later Permian reptiles were somewhat similar to mammals in their stance, teeth pattern, and appearance, and included rabbitlike *Dicynodon*, wolflike *Lycaenops*, and molelike *Cistecephalus*.

▽ By the Triassic Period, reptiles had developed into many different types. The mammal-like reptiles were still around and included hippopotamus-like *Lystrosaurus*.

The big difference between a reptile and an amphibian is that the reptile lays an egg with a protective covering. Inside, a membrane and fluid allow the developing animal to breathe air. It does not need to live in water.

The following Permian Period was a time of deserts and ice caps. The amphibians adapted to the dry climate by evolving into armored land-living types. It was the reptiles, though, that did best in the drier condition. The main reptile types of that time were mammal-like. They had straight, not sprawling, walking legs, and different-sized teeth like a mammal's.

In the Triassic, the deserts continued. The big amphibians died out. The mammal-like reptiles faded away, but not before the first mammals evolved from them. The thecodonts became most important, evolving into several groups, including the dinosaurs.

# LATE TRIASSIC PERIOD
245 to 208 million years ago

Conifer

Horsetails

*Desmatosuchus*

*Rutiodon*

In the Late Triassic Period, the first phase of the Age of Dinosaurs, the desert conditions still existed over much of our planet. All the continents of the world were jammed together to make up one huge landmass, called Pangaea. This supercontinent was so big that most of it was a long way from the moist winds of the sea, and so hot dry conditions were common. The earlier Permian Period had been a time of mountains, formed as all the separate continents crashed into one another. By the Triassic Period these mountains were mostly worn down to hills.

Ferns

The animals living in this ancient landscape consisted of the last of the mammal-like reptiles. Among them were *Placerias,* thecodonts such as armored *Desmatosuchus,* and crocodile-like *Rutiodon*. There were also the earliest dinosaurs, for example *Coelophysis*.

Placerias

Mountain ranges were still growing up along the edges of the continents. From the young Rocky Mountains, streams tumbled downward and spread rubble and sand over what is now Arizona. Along the routes of these rivers grew groups of conifer trees and cycadeoids, which were plants with swollen trunks that looked like the modern cycads. The small plants covering the ground of these woodlands were mainly ferns. Reed-beds of horsetails lined the riverbanks.

How do we know all this? The remains of all these plants now lie in Petrified Forest National Park in Arizona. The logs of the conifers, turned to stone, lie in the desert landscape where the overlying rock has been worn away by the weather.

In what is now South America, fast-running dinosaurs like *Staurikosaurus* evolved. In Europe lived *Plateosaurus*, the first big dinosaur.

△ In an area that is now Arizona grew conifers, cycadeoids, ferns, and giant horsetails. The dinosaur *Coelophysis*, seen here among the trees, lived alongside crocodile- and mammal-like reptiles.

Coelophysis

19

# EARLY AND MIDDLE JURASSIC PERIOD

208 to 157 million years ago

In the early part of the Jurassic Period the supercontinent of Pangaea was still intact. It would not be long, though, before it would begin to split apart. Splits in the land began to form along the line that would tear North America away from Africa.

Shallow seas began to spread across the surface of Pangaea. These brought much more moist climates far inland on the continent, and forests flourished where once there had been deserts. The seas flooded the low land between North America and Africa.

At that time, much of Britain and the continent of Europe consisted of low islands in a shallow sea. Sea reptiles, such as sleek dolphinlike *Ichthyosaurus* and the long-necked *Plesiosaurus,* chased fish and the coil-shelled ammonites in the warm, shallow waters. The islands would have been covered by a plant life looking like that of the Triassic Period. The early armored dinosaur *Scelidosaurus* lived here, and had to guard itself against big meat-eaters, while pterosaurs circled in the sky overhead.

At the other end of Pangaea, where South Africa now lies, there were plant-eating dinosaurs like *Heterodontosaurus* and *Massospondylus,* and meat-eating kinds like *Syntarsus.*

▷ Southern England about 165 million years ago. A *Plesiosaurus* hauls itself up onto the beach, alongside a dead *Ichthyosaurus.* A big meat-eating dinosaur, left, and a *Scelidosaurus*, right, are nearby. *Dimorphodon* fly overhead.

Big meat-eater related to *Megalosaurus*

Plesiosaurus

Dimorphodon

Scelidosaurus

Ichthyosaurus

21

# LATE JURASSIC PERIOD
## 157 to 146 million years ago

As the Middle Jurassic Period gave way to the Late Jurassic, the supercontinent of Pangaea began slowly to be pulled apart. The shallow seas continued to spread over the low-lying areas. One particular sea, now called the Sundance Sea, spread southward over the continent of North America. It cut off the new Rocky Mountains to the west from the main part of the continent to the east. Sand and pebbles spread out into the sea from the foot of the mountains and formed a broad river plain. In spite of the nearby sea, this plain was quite dry.

▽ Plant-eating dinosaurs, meat-eating dinosaurs, and pterosaurs lived in and around a coniferous forest on a dry plain in Colorado.

*Cornodactylus*

*Allosaurus*

*Stegosaurus*

*Ornitholestes*

Apatosaurus

Brachiosaurus

Ceratosaurus

Mesadactylus

Plants grew in large numbers only along the courses of the many streams. The rocks formed here consist of sandstones, mudstones, and siltstones in a great sequence of layers called the Morrison Formation. Parts of the edges of the layers can be seen in Montana, Utah, Colorado, and New Mexico.

The Morrison Formation is so rich in dinosaur remains that it was the site of great dinosaur hunts in the years between 1877 and 1900. The fossils discovered allow us to imagine the open plain, with forests of conifers and ferns along the waterways, inhabited by big plant-eating dinosaurs like *Apatosaurus* and *Brachiosaurus,* and armored dinosaurs like *Stegosaurus*. These were hunted and killed by meat-eaters like *Ceratosaurus* and *Allosaurus*. Smaller meat-eaters and pterosaurs were there, too.

# EARLY CRETACEOUS PERIOD
146 to 97 million years ago

In Early Cretaceous times the split-up of Pangaea was well underway. An ocean had opened up between North America and Africa, although North America and Europe were still joined in the north. Africa and South America were still one landmass, but Antarctica and India had broken away as islands. At the beginning the shallow seas covering northern Europe had gone. A large freshwater lake, the Wealden, was left over southern England and northern France. Around it were ridges of limestone rock formed in the Carboniferous Period, and to the north lay an even older mountain range.

▽ Herds of *Iguanodon* and of *Hypsilophodon* move through the rich vegetation of what is now southeast England.

*Iguanodon*

*Hylaeosaurus*

24

*Ornithodesmus*

*Baryonyx*

*Hypsilophodon*

The dinosaurs that lived around the Wealden lake included *Iguanodon*. It seems to have lived in herds, feeding on horsetail plants. We sometimes find *Iguanodon* footprints in the mudstone, along with skin marks showing where these dinosaurs wallowed in the mud. Living there also were swift-footed *Hypsilophodon,* meat-eating or fish-eating *Baryonyx,* and armored *Hylaeosaurus*. Big pterosaurs, such as *Ornithodesmus,* flew overhead, and early mammals scampered in the ferny undergrowth.

The muds and clays laid down in the Wealden lake are known as the Wealden Formation. They contain fossils of conifer trees, ferns, tree ferns, ginkgoes, and early flowering plants, as well as the animals of the time. Mud cracks and rain pits in the mudstones show where the shallow waters dried out from time to time.

# LATE CRETACEOUS PERIOD
97 to 65 million years ago

By the Late Cretaceous Period, the end of the Age of Dinosaurs, Pangaea had ceased to exist; the supercontinent had completely broken up. North America was separate from South America and from Europe, and Africa had broken away from South America. However, Antarctica and Australia were still joined, and western North America was connected to northeastern Asia by a land bridge. Many places were covered by shallow seas. A broad shallow sea, the Niobrara Sea, cut North America completely in two from north to south.

▽ Heavily wooded landscape in what is now Wyoming. Herds of *Edmontosaurus* move across country, keeping well clear of *Tyrannosaurus*. Modern-looking birds fly overhead.

*Edmontosaurus*

*Ankylosaurus*

*Triceratops*

*Thescelosaurus*

Tyrannosaurus

Leptoceratops

Plant life was changing everywhere. The huge forests of conifer trees and ferns were being replaced by modern-looking forests of oak and willow. Flowering plants formed the undergrowth. Palm trees grew in the warmer areas. The region that today is Wyoming had such a forest, browsed by herds of two-footed plant-eaters like huge *Edmontosaurus,* horned dinosaurs like *Triceratops* and *Leptoceratops,* and armored giants like *Ankylosaurus.* These were all preyed upon by the great meat-eater *Tyrannosaurus.* The remains of these dinosaurs have been found in the rock layers of the Lance Formation.

# THE RISE OF MAMMALS

The dinosaurs and many other creatures died out suddenly about 65 million years ago, a time that marks the end of the Cretaceous Period. We do not know why this happened. Possibly the moving continents changed the climates too much; the weather became too hot or cold. Maybe diseases spread through the whole dinosaur kingdom. Or perhaps these animals could not cope with the changing plant life. Another possibility is that there was some kind of great disaster. Perhaps the Earth was struck by a giant meteorite. Whatever occurred, the dinosaurs all perished, along with the other great reptiles of the time.

After all the big reptiles were wiped out, the little mammals that had played such a minor part for the previous 160 million years suddenly became important.

The pterosaurs, the flying reptiles, were replaced by winged mammals, the bats. The ichthyosaurs were eventually replaced by swimming mammals, the whales. The different types of dinosaurs—the meat-eaters and the plant-eaters big and small—were replaced by all kinds of meat- and plant-eating mammals. These spread from tropical forests, through deserts to the polar wilderness. The birds, too, spread out and became much more important than they were before.

At first most mammals were forest-living types, but soon the forests gave way to grassy plains. Plains-living mammals later evolved, with long running legs and strong grass-eating teeth. These were the ancestors of the horses and the antelopes. It was the Age of Mammals in which we are living now.

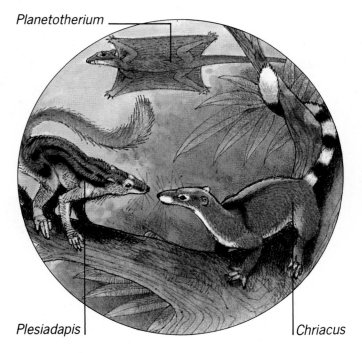

Planetotherium

Plesiadapis

Chriacus

**Paleocene times 65 to 56.5 million years ago**
The Paleocene forests were home to tree-living mammals like climbing *Plesiadapis* and *Chriacus*, and gliding *Planetotherium*.

Uintatherium

Hyrachyus

Hyracotherium

**Eocene times 56.5 to 35.5 million years ago**
In the Eocene forests lived huge rhinoceros-like *Uintatherium*, the little rhinoceros *Hyrachyus*, and the tiny earliest horse *Hyracotherium*.

## The Age of Humans

The dinosaurs dominated the Earth for long ages. Today human beings do. All the known history of human beings is measured in thousands of years. The emergence of human beings—unique, self-conscious creatures—is a mystery. Scientists are tracking down physical clues like the similarity of other "hominids" (shown here) and man. There is much still to be learned; you may help learn it.

*Brontotherium*

*Megatylopus*

*Hyaenodon*

*Pliohippus*

*Epigaulus*

*Amebelodon*

*Synthetoceras*

*Archaeotherium*

*Hoplophoneus*

**Oligocene times 35.5 to 23.5 million years ago**
The open landscapes of the Oligocene Epoch had big plant-eaters, *Brontotherium* and *Archaeotherium*, and meat-eating *Hyaenodon* and *Hoplophoneus*.

**Miocene times 23.5 to 5.2 million years ago**
The Miocene grasslands had the horse *Pliohippus*, gazellelike *Synthetoceras*, the camel *Megatylopus*, the rodent *Epigaulus*, and the elephant *Amebelodon*.

29

# DO YOU KNOW?

## When did the dinosaurs first appear?

The earliest dinosaurs we presently know are *Herrerasaurus* and *Staurikosaurus*. These meat-eaters lived at the start of the Late Triassic Period in South America; they evolved from the crocodile-like thecodonts about 225 million years ago.

## When did the dinosaurs die out?

Dinosaurs became extinct at the very end of the Cretaceous Period, about 65 million years ago. For a few million years before this the numbers of dinosaurs had been getting smaller, but then suddenly all these animals, and many others, died out.

## How are dinosaurs named?

A dinosaur's proper scientific name (in fact the proper scientific name for all animals) consists of two parts. The first part, the *genus* name, has a capital letter. The second part, the *species* name, does not. Both names are written in italics. Very similar species or kinds of dinosaurs are grouped together in the same genus. That is why we sometimes talk about *Tyrannosaurus rex*. More often we just use the genus name, such as *Tyrannosaurus*.

## How many kinds of dinosaurs were there?

It has been estimated that the total number of dinosaur genera (*genera* is the plural of *genus*) that ever lived is between 900 and 1,200. Scientists think that they have discovered about a quarter of the genera that existed.

## Which area had the most kinds of dinosaurs?

Triassic, Jurassic, and Cretaceous rocks of western Canada and western United States contain remains of possibly the largest number of different kinds of dinosaurs. They include meat-eaters *Dilophosaurus, Allosaurus,* and *Coelophysis*, long-necked plant-eaters like *Apatosaurus* and *Brachiosaurus*, two-footed plant-eaters such as *Stygimoloch* and *Corythosaurus*, armored *Euoplocephalus* and plated *Stegosaurus,* and the horned *Triceratops*.

## Which were the most widely ranging dinosaurs?

*Iguanodon,* from the United States, Europe, and Mongolia, was likely to have been the most widespread. Other widely distributed dinosaurs included *Brachiosaurus* from Colorado and Tanzania, *Pachyrhinosaurus* from Alberta and Alaska, *Psittacosaurus* from China, Mongolia, and Siberia, and *Chasmosaurus* from Texas and Alberta.

## Which were the most southerly dinosaurs?

Scientists have found dinosaur remains in Early Cretaceous rocks of southeastern Australia. These include the armored *Minmi* and two-footed plant-eaters *Fulgurotherium, Leaellynasaura,* and *Atlascopcosaurus*. In Early Cretaceous times this part of Australia lay well within the Antarctic Circle. Dinosaur fossils have also been found in Antarctica, but scientists are not yet sure which species these come from.

## Which were the most northerly dinosaurs?

Duckbilled dinosaur remains have been found in Late Cretaceous rocks in Alaska. In Late Cretaceous times this area would have been hundreds of miles farther north than it is today. Footprints like those of *Iguanodon* have been found in Early Cretaceous rocks of the Arctic Islands of Spitzbergen.

# GLOSSARY

**algae** a very primitive type of plant, such as a seaweed.

**ammonites** an ancient group of shelled animals, related to modern squid, cuttlefish, and octopuses. They died out at the same time as the dinosaurs.

**amphibians** animals such as frogs, toads, newts, and salamanders, which lay their eggs and live as young in water but as adults can live on land.

**climates** the average weather conditions in different parts of the world.

**colonization** the way in which a new type of plant or animal gradually takes over a new living area.

**conifer trees** trees that produce seeds in cones—for example, pines, firs, and larches. Their needlelike leaves usually stay on the trees all year.

**continents** the huge areas of land, or landmasses, on Earth. The modern continents are, in order of size, Asia, Africa, North America, South America, Antarctica, Europe, and Australia.

**core** the innermost part of the Earth, probably made of iron. The inner core is probably solid and the outer core is liquid.

**crust** the outer skin of the Earth.

**cycadeoids** ancient plants with swollen trunks that resembled the modern cycads, which are tropical plants that look like palm trees but have fernlike leaves.

**evolved** changed, from generation to generation, producing a new species.

**fossils** parts or traces of once-living plants or animals that are preserved in the rocks.

**geography** the study of the appearance, formation, and changes to the land, sea, and air on Earth. A major branch of geography is geology, the science of rocks, minerals and fossils.

**ginkgoes** trees that look like conifers but with leaves that are shed in the fall. There is only one living species, the Maidenhair tree.

**Gondwana** the southern section of the ancient continent of Pangaea, consisting of what is now South America, Africa, India, Australia, and Antarctica.

**horsetails** plants, related to ferns, with sprays of green branches along an upright stem and tiny leaves.

**Laurasia** the northern section of Pangaea, consisting of what is now North America, Europe, and most of Asia.

**lungfish** fish that have lungs as well as gills and so can breathe air. They can survive droughts or live in stagnant waters.

**mammals** vertebrate animals that produce live young and feed them on milk. Modern mammals include cats, dogs, mice, monkeys, and ourselves.

**mantle** the stony layer that makes up the bulk of the Earth. It is solid but with a soft layer near the top.

**molecules** the smallest particles of chemical compounds formed by the joining together of atoms, the building units of all matter.

**Ornithischia** the bird-hipped dinosaurs, including the two-footed plant-eaters, the plated dinosaurs, the armored dinosaurs, and the horned dinosaurs.

**ornithopod** a two-footed plant-eating dinosaur, such as *Iguanodon*.

**Pangaea** the name given to the supercontinent that once existed, in which all the continental masses of the Earth were joined together.

**reptiles** vertebrate animals generally with a dry, scaly skin that lay shelled eggs. Living reptiles include lizards and turtles.

**Saurischia** the lizard-hipped dinosaurs, including the meat-eaters and the long-necked plant-eaters.

**sauropod** a long-necked plant-eating dinosaur, such as *Apatosaurus*.

**species** a collection of animals, or any living things, in which individuals look like one another and can breed with each other to produce young. Breeding, reproduction, and mating are all terms to describe the process by which individuals make more of their species.

**theropod** a meat-eating dinosaur, such as *Tyrannosaurus*.

**vertebrates** animals that have a backbone. This includes the fish, amphibians, reptiles, birds, and mammals. As mammals, we are also vertebrates.

# INDEX

**ACKNOWLEDGMENTS**

**Picture credits**
Pages 14-15 C.A. Henley/Biofotos

**Artwork credits**
Chris Forsey: pages 1, 2-3, 18-19, 20-21, 22-23, 24-25, 26-27. James G. Robins:
pages 4-5, 6-7, 8-9, 14-15, 16-17, 28-29. Dennys Ovenden: pages 16-17, 29
Hayward Art Group: 10-11, 12-13 and all diagrams. Steve Kirk: cover illustration.